My Healing Heart

A Monthly Account of the
First Year of Grieving

To Myra
With the hope
that your heart will
soon start to heal
Bobbie

Barbara Cheris

Pen and Ink Drawings by Heidi Cheris

To my daughters, Heidi and Lori,

and my grandchildren,

Ariana, Jake, Alex, Noah, and Logan,

who carry David's spirit with them into the future,

ensuring his immortality.

THE FIRST MONTH

MAY

I am at my husband's funeral and I am in a hostess mode, greeting everyone as they stand in line to pay their respects. I recall old times together; I introduce acquaintances to my children; I thank them for coming; I am an actress on a stage, not a widow in mourning. I give the eulogy without breaking down in tears, for it is I who knew David best and can know best what to say. With words I restore dignity to this wonderful man, a dignity which his illness stole from him. My two daughters, Heidi and Lori, and my son-in-law, Phillip, also speak, each one conveying a different side of David, helping to complete the picture of this man and the influence he had on us all. I listen sadly, attentively, but do not cry. My tears can wait for a more private moment.

Later, I greet relatives, friends, and some of David's colleagues from the hospital where he worked as a radiologist for thirty-four years. I make sure everyone is well fed, that out-oftowners have a ride back to the airport, and that I have had a chance to chat with everyone who has come back to my brother's house, where I am staying. Everyone says how strong I am, what a beautiful service it was, what a huge turnout at our synagogue. One woman tells me it was the most beautiful funeral she's ever attended. I think, "How can a funeral be beautiful?" The two words are an oxymoron, a discordant note which jars me. The funeral has gone well, but David is in the ground, and I am beginning the first month of my grieving.

All week I greet friends and family who come to pay the *shiva* call, the week of mourning in the Jewish religion. I am in control and able to listen to stories about David and even to engage in a somewhat normal chit-chat. Then, I return to my home in Boston and begin my life alone as a widow.

I walk into the house and hear a deafening silence. As I look around, images of the last year and a half keep flashing through my mind. I remember the shocking diagnosis of incurable, metastatic colon cancer. I have flashbacks of David's surgery, the months of chemotherapy, and the many weeks he

was bedridden upstairs under Hospice care with me as his primary caregiver. And I recall David's last selfless and remarkable gift to me and the reason I'm here in Boston: When David
found out he was dying, he told me he wanted to spend his
remaining time helping me resettle to wherever I wanted to be
when I would be alone. I knew I needed the emotional support
of being near a daughter, and I wanted David to get the best
available medical care. So, within a couple of months of his
diagnosis, we had sold our home on Cazenovia Lake in upstate
New York and moved to Boston. All these changes have hap-
pened to me so fast, and now I stand here in this house as a
widow.

I walk into our bedroom and can *see* David lying in the
hospital bed, even though the bed is no longer there. I almost
trip on it as I cross the room to look inside our closet. I finger
his clothes: a favorite argyle, cashmere sweater, some leather,
woven suspenders, a funky, colorful vest he bought in Mexico,
his white, hospital lab coat with his name embroidered in red
on the pocket. I rub his old moccasin shoes, taking notice of the

shape his wide feet made in the leather. At last, I can cry. I lie

crumpled on the closet floor, with memories all around me, and

the tears are freely flowing. The silence is broken, and the sound

I hear is my sobbing. Tonight, I climb into our bed and auto-

matically slide over to David's side, burying my head in his

pillow. I can smell my husband's presence. Suddenly, I am so

tired, and I sleep.

I am glad that I have so much to do this first month. The

lawyers keep sending me forms to fill out and try to explain

documents and trusts which in legalese make me break out in

hives. I take Phil to all the meetings, as he can make sense of it

all and will, perhaps, give me a crash course in financial and

estate planning at a later date.

David has left everything as organized as possible for me,

but still it's a paper and emotional overload. One day, I am

searching through our file cabinet to find a health form, so I

look inside a folder labeled "important papers." Inside, is a

Motor Trend magazine, telling about Avanti cars, an old clas-

sic car David once owned. I burst out laughing, thinking of

David's unique filing system. Of course, he would file this under "important." When I search for wills, I do not find it under "W," but rather under the law firm which drew it up. There is a method in this madness. I want to tell David I like his filing system and am beginning to understand it. I miss him so much and need to talk to him right now. Death is so final, and I'm not ready for it. How did it creep up on us like this?

I walk around the house staring at all the photos of us and the children and grandchildren. I want to turn back the clock to a time when we were all happy and carefree, a time before cancer. In my head I label all the pictures *before* cancer or *after* cancer and I want to return to the *before* cancer time with some kind of a magic wand. I can't believe I ever was carefree, without this terrible weight that I feel inside me. Will it ever get better?

Meanwhile, the cards and donations to Hospice keep piling up, and I am occupied answering them all with a personal note of thanks. I am so touched by the outpouring of love from his department staff. I learn from their letters to me how much he helped them through their own crises in life, a side which David did not even totally share with me. He had been a father figure to many, it seems, and I am not the only one mourning his death. He had an extended family at work, and these warm, loving people are now letting me know how much they care.

At the same time, I am becoming angry and resentful at some of my closest friends back home. Now that I am not totally occupied as a caregiver for David, I have time to think and to reflect, and it bothers me that so many could not cope with his illness and death and chose to keep us at a distance, physically and emotionally. I am so disappointed and hurt that more trips weren't made to Boston to see David before he died. How he would have loved to spend more time chatting with a good buddy. Some did make the effort. My brother and sister-in-law drove to Boston every weekend as David grew weaker, and my brother sat with him, joked with him, listened to him, helped to care for him. One couple from back home drove to Boston to spend a weekend with us a few months before his death. A friend from childhood, who also went through medical school with him, flew to Boston to spend a day at his side. A close friend from work called and e-mailed him regularly, and they began to sign their e-mails "with love."

This same friend sent me a poem about David which I have framed and read often, always with tears. Friends from Atlanta came to spend a few days to be near him just a few weeks before he died. Others did not. They said the weather was not good for traveling, or they, themselves, were not feeling well. I had to listen to a list of symptoms from some of my friends who made it seem as if David were in an illness competition with them. I feel my disappointment and anger build up.

Signs of spring are all over. Buds on trees are opening and flowers are bursting from the ground. Year after year they will continue this cycle of life, and I feel a resentment at how easily and predictably nature springs back to life each season, while my husband lies forever still under the earth.

I find resentment, too, in the changes in my life: new people and places that David did not know. I don't really want to meet anyone new, buy anything new or travel anywhere he hasn't been. I feel that if I can keep the world the same all around me, he will somehow seem closer, and I won't loosen the bond I have with him. The old friends are the ones he knew. My old clothes are the ones he saw me wear. I even keep up the same routine as to when I go to bed and when I get up and which seat I take at the kitchen table and which television programs I watch. I don't want anything to change, even though everything has changed. I don't like the bitterness and resentment inside me, but it's there. I am somehow getting through this first month and keeping busy.

THE SECOND MONTH

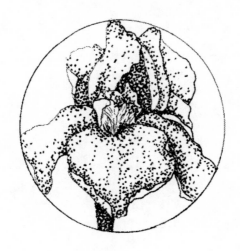

JUNE

I am taking my first solo airplane trip as a widow, so that I can see my new grandson in California. Logan was born just a week before David's death, and although he never got to see him, he did know that he had been born. It's strange how different I feel traveling alone now. Before David was ill, I had traveled to California without him when I was needed to help out with the grandchildren and David couldn't get away. Then, the trip didn't bother me. Now that I am a new widow, I can barely stand to walk through the airport. I imagine everyone is a family or a pair going on vacation. I sit on the plane, trying to bury my head in a book, but concentrating only on my own sadness, remembering all the trips David and I had taken.

During my week in California, Lori drops me off at a mall one day for a couple of hours. I enter the mall through a store I usually walk through, passing through the men's department, and I start to panic. I see flashbacks of David and me picking out sweaters together. It is so painful for me to see displays of men's clothing, and I rush to a phone and try to reach Lori to tell her to please come and get me. I do okay if I spend my time with Lori and my son-in-law, Morgan, and my grandchildren in their surroundings. Yet, I cannot visit the beach where David and I spent so much time together, and I cannot go to our favorite restaurant. While I make it through the week, I realize how raw I am inside.

Back in Boston, I enter a drugstore to buy a few notions, and I watch a woman stocking up on a canned nutritional supplement and questioning the pharmacist as to how long it will take to get her husband's prescription filled. She's obviously in a hurry to get back to him. I don't know this woman or even if her husband is very sick, but I am suddenly reliving David's illness and remembering all the times I stood by impatiently waiting for his prescriptions and stocking up on nutritional supplies. Unexpectedly, my eyes well up with tears, and I rush out of the store.

My wounds are reopened, sometimes unexpectedly like in

the drugstore and sometimes, predictably, like whenever I'm driving the car, listening to some beautiful music or looking out of the car window at water and spot a motorboat or canoe. Then, I think of us and our yesterdays living at the lake in Cazenovia, and the tears run down my cheeks while I am driving alone.

Today, while walking through a mall, I become hungry, so I impulsively stop into a restaurant for supper before I head home. I am very uncomfortable sitting here alone, gazing at couples and groups dining together. I remember what David had once said to me when we were out eating together and spotted a lone diner at a table near us: "See that woman over there? She's just *pretending* to read that paper! She's probably lonely." I want to tell David, "You're right. She *is* lonely, and that woman is now *me*." I eat my meal in about five minutes, ask for the check, and quickly leave. Until my mood changes, I will avoid dining alone in any restaurant.

Hospice has sent a volunteer to meet with me once a week for the first thirteen months of my grieving process. I am a very private person, and it is not easy for me to open up my heart to anyone. I feel so lucky to have met Susan, my hospice volunteer, who, coincidentally, is a professional social worker. She senses so well what to say, how to listen, and how to respond as we discuss my emotions and progress each week. She also happens to come from upstate New York, not too great a distance from where David and I lived. I laugh with her as I tell her funny and unique stories about David. Often, I burst into tears, as I relate to her how much I miss my husband and how hard it is for me to navigate through life without him by my side. But she's such a good listener, and I feel a catharsis in the talking.

She is also the first middle-aged friend I've made since my move to Boston, and I realize how important that is. Because I have spent almost all of my last year and a half taking care of David and because Boston is a new city to me where I have no friends, Susan suggests that I also join a bereavement group at a nearby hospital. That way, I'll meet other adults who are going through the same emotions as I.

So, I start going once a week to a bereavement group therapy program run by Paula, a gentle, compassionate therapist. I enter this group of about a dozen adults, mostly women, all of us in varying states of progress in our bereavement. Paula keeps a box of tissues on a small table in the center of the room, and we all sit in a circle telling our stories each week. I am always reaching for the tissues as I talk about my week. I notice that it's easy for me to talk and easy for me to cry in front of these new friends. For some of them, it's not easy to cry or to talk. Each of us copes differently and at a different pace, I guess. Some of the people have been coming for as long as two years and still find it hard to open up.

THE THIRD MONTH

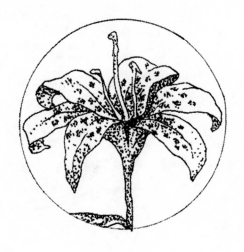

JULY

One of the hardest *firsts* to get through is coming up this month. I dread the Fourth of July, since that was a day we celebrated with a huge party at our home every year for twenty-five years. Our village of Cazenovia puts on a small fireworks display over the lake that David and I always thought must be the most special and exciting fireworks display anywhere, barring none. He would take the little ones out on his boat so they could see the dazzling display up close and overhead.

This year Heidi, Phil, my grandchildren, Jake and Noah, and I go to the rooftop of the Boston Museum of Science for their Fourth of July celebration with food and crafts and the music of the Boston Pops piped in and a wonderful view of a spectacular fireworks display overhead. Early in the evening I am in a good mood and enjoying the festivities and watching the children get their faces painted with firecracker symbols and stars and stripes. Everything is fine until later when I look skyward and see the first fireworks start to explode. I feel as if my heart is exploding, too, and the tears start streaming down my cheeks, though I remain silent. Fortunately, it is dark outside and the grandchildren's eyes are focused skyward, so they do not witness their grandma's despair. The Fourth of July ends as does another *first* in my year of getting through all the *firsts*.

I can tell this is going to be a rough month for me. Today I hear a crashing sound coming from the basement. I discover that an entire rack of David's clothes in the cedar closet has fallen down and the rod has come completely unhinged from the wall. Obviously, I have overloaded it with heavy clothes. I call a nephew who lives nearby and he comes over to help in reattaching the support. When I look at my large nephew and I look at David's clothes in a heap, I realize that they would be a perfect fit. My nephew asks me if I am sure I want to part with David's things. I tell him there are a few special items I can not part with, but he can have anything else he wants. So a collapsed closet rod turns out to be the motivating force which helps me make this decision. Those things which Steve, my nephew, doesn't want will go to charity. I don't want to think about it anymore.

Today I carry armloads of clothes to Goodwill and force myself to do it quickly and not involve Heidi in helping me carry her dad's clothes. I try to be dispassionate about it all, but I must say that it feels as if I am throwing out part of David when I leave the clothes to be given away. It's a feeling of finality. I hate it! I know he's not coming back, but I need to keep some of his favorite items of clothing around just to remind me of the past which I yearn for. Another weepy day.

Susan phones me one day this week to reschedule a visit and finds me sounding sad. I tell her I'm in the bedroom stuffing David's socks, underwear, and pajamas into bags to bring to Goodwill. She says she'll be right over. I can't believe how wonderful she is to drop everything and rush over to help me. She and I sit on the bedroom floor, sorting things into bags and talking about David. Between tears, I tell her some funny anecdotes about him. Susan insists on delivering the bags herself.

She said I should never have dropped his clothing off by myself. I feel relieved that I don't have to go. I open the treasure
box in my closet and share some of David's letters with her. I
want her to understand the remarkable man I'm talking about.
Here is an unscheduled, impromptu visit by a hospice volunteer who has turned out to be my savior and friend.

In my bereavement group I am noticing some differences in
the way I am coping from the way most of the others do. Almost everybody else has to constantly keep on the go; "keep
busy," they say; "that's the secret." Also, many come home
only to "flop in bed," as one man comments. He hates to be in
his house. He still can't sit in his wife's chair, even after several
months. His daughters have been supplying him with meals
every day for months now. Another man tells us that no matter
how busy he is, it still amounts to coming home to an empty
house at the end of the day, and that is the saddest, loneliest
time. One of the women says it took her quite awhile before
she could stay in her house, so she stayed with her daughter for
the first few months following her husband's death. Still, an-

other in our group sold her home soon after her husband died, and moved into another home to escape some of the memories.

But I find a soothing comfort in my home and all the familiar things which surround me. I look around and each object has a special meaning to me: an antique we bought on a trip together, or some gift David surprised me with, or a favorite painting of ours, or the grandfather clock he picked out for his sixtieth birthday, or the tools strewn on top of his workbench as if he were about to return any minute to use them, and a forceps thrown into the toolbox, a tool only a doctor would use. It makes me smile. I'm glad we lived together in this house in Boston, even for too short a time. It makes the house more personal to me, and I know he knows where I am. I feel his presence here.

Some things are sad to keep, but I still need to do so. I still keep his wallet, his passport, his eyeglasses, his collection of watches, his keys, even his favorite, old floor lamp which he studied under in medical school days. Sometimes, I peer into his soft, worn wallet and study all the identification cards he carried: his medical license, his driver's license, his social security card, and all the other cards of a man who no longer walks this earth.

I have put all the letters David wrote me since I was nineteen years old into my special treasure box, and sometimes I sit alone on the closet floor reading those letters from long ago. I read them forward from the first letter he ever wrote me, and I read them back again in time from the last one he wrote me, a love letter on my birthday almost exactly a year before his death. In it, he acknowledges that "we are in a battle we will not ultimately win but we will try. Winning," he writes, "is really getting the most time and the most out of the time we get for each other." He adds, "This is our battle and I couldn't have a better partner." Each time I read his letters I weep, but I feel so close and connected to him when I hear the words I am reading, and I feel compelled to read them and be reminded of how much he loved me.

I don't want to spend most of my time away from this house. I refuse to join activities or organizations I'm not interested in, just for the sake of keeping busy. Maybe, I'll do some gardening; maybe, I'll start baking again. These are activities I have always liked. We'll see. I don't feel pressured.

Every week I ask Susan how I'm doing. She says she can tell from my physical appearance that I seem to be doing well. She sees me *put together*, always with makeup and jewelry. She doesn't see me, as Heidi often does, wearing the same jeans or sweatpants over and over again, day after day. Susan asks me if I would ever want to just stay in my robe all day long and not leave the house. I tell her that sounds like a good idea, something I would love to do, but only for a day once every now and then. It would be so nice to shut out the world and rest and not answer the phone for a day or two. I feel so enervated. Maybe, someday I'll do that, just pull the blanket up and stay in bed and pretend I'm not home to the rest of the world.

THE FOURTH MONTH

AUGUST

Something strange is happening to me. Sometimes, I feel as if David is still beside me, whispering in my ear. I find myself becoming more assertive, more spontaneous in my expressions and somewhat stronger emotionally. It is as if much of his strength and wisdom has been implanted in me and did not simply go to the grave with him. I blurt out advice and criticism to my family members when I feel it is in their best interest, and I assert myself more often when I think it is in my best interest. David's expressions and direct, frank way of speaking come out of my mouth without my even thinking about it. I've definitely become less inhibited in a positive way. After all that I have been through, I do not care to *walk on eggs* with others.

I have become more vocal in advocating my rights on behalf of a business venture David was involved with along with several other physicians. I feel they may not be honoring a contractual commitment, and I enlist the help of my attorneys to make sure the letter of the law is followed. I do it for my benefit, but I feel even stronger about David getting fair treatment from this group, even though it is done posthumously. This week, I also called my stock broker and told him I have decided that he is not the right person to be handling my financial affairs, even though he has done so for forty years. I explain that my needs are different now, and that I have made a decision as to how my finances will be handled and by whom. I have thought all this out and discussed it with my lawyers and my son-in-law, Phil, and feel a self-empowerment that I never expressed before. I am as diplomatic as I can be in my dealings with people, but I say what I feel.

I am benefiting from my bereavement group each week and enjoying the camaraderie of the others. We are all helpless as far as knowing how we as individuals can best cope with our losses. Yet, as a group we are understanding and able to give counsel and common-sense suggestions to one another. I suppose it's always easier to see the right thing to do for someone else. I am making friends among the group and have one or two people I can call upon if I want to go out for dinner or to a movie.

There are still many days when I get very weepy and feel sorry for myself. I miss so many things. I miss David's smile and gaze. I miss his laughter. I miss having him know what I am thinking just by looking at me. I miss holding hands. I miss his arms around me. I miss our intimacies. It has been so long since I felt that passion. I miss slow dancing with him, feeling his body close to mine, and I miss our old fashioned, fifties-style jitterbugging, where he'd swing me about and pull me back toward him in our familiar, repetitive way. And I miss the simplest pleasure of watching a video in bed with him with a big bowl of popcorn between us. Tonight I rent a video, make a bowl of popcorn, and watch the movie while cuddling next to Annie, my sweet, twenty-five pound, blind dog, whom I've had for twelve years.

It really helps to have Annie. She sleeps snuggled next to me each night. I have someone warm to touch and hug and kiss. I can talk out loud to someone in the house. Otherwise, I think I would go crazy. My little blind dog is such a comfort!

One friend, who is in my bereavement group, says she always leaves most of the lights on in her house when she goes out in the evening, as she can't stand coming home to a dark house at night. Many of the women seem to have varying degrees of this fear of approaching an empty house, especially at night. With Annie, I never walk into an empty house. I always leave the kitchen light on for her when I go out, even though she can't see. Maybe, I'm doing it out of habit or maybe I'm doing it for me, but I know that my fear of returning home is certainly lessened with a dog in the house, even though she's so helpless herself.

THE FIFTH MONTH

SEPTEMBER

This month I am attending my niece's wedding back in upstate New York. Outwardly, I am confident, cheerful, and strong. The wedding is held at a club on Cazenovia Lake, but the ceremony has to be held indoors, since the weather is inclement. I'm glad that I can be inside and not have to gaze out at the lake and all the memories it represents. At the reception I try not to be bothered by couples dancing, and I take my two little grandsons, one at a time, out on the dance floor for a swing dance. I'm coping okay.

My friends tell me how well I look. They all inquire as to how I am doing. Who am I to burst their bubble or to turn them off by relating my loneliness? I answer with a smile, "I'm doing okay" or "It's rough, but I'm putting one foot in front of the other." People get tired of hearing anyone whine about their lot in life, and there is always someone with more problems than I. Others expect the grieving to be over by now or think that I have *snapped out of it* by now. I had a long, happy marriage. I have a lot to be thankful for. I shouldn't complain, so I try not to, except when I am alone with my thoughts or with a friend who is going through the same thing. Then, I am free to grieve.

Just before leaving town, I go to the cemetery with my children, grandchildren, and my brother and have an intimate unveiling of David's monument. For the first time, I see David's name etched in marble and read the year he was born and the year he died. It seems surreal standing by his grave. I don't feel his presence here. I feel his presence inside of me when I am away from the cemetery.

Lori reads a poem she has written, and it is incredibly touching. Something she says haunts me. She tells about wanting to dream of her father but being unable to do so. I, too, feel this void. Why does he not yet appear in my dreams, even though so many other, trivial people and events appear in my silly, senseless dreams? I want to hear his voice and see him move about in my dreams at least. *Forever* is such a long time not to see someone again. I cannot even remember the exact color of his eyes, those eyes I gazed into for so many years. I used to know.

When he was dying, I tried to memorize his every feature. I stared at him and studied him so often and for so long, and now his features are fading in my mind, and I don't want them to. As painful as it is, I try to think back, but the cancer period is more vivid than all of our forty-three years together.

Sometimes, I play a game with myself and try to think back to what day I would choose if I could be granted just one day back in time. Would I choose a holiday, Thanksgiving, perhaps, when our whole family was gathered around the table, chatting, eating, and laughing a lot? Would I pick a time when we were off on vacation to some remote and scenic spot? No, I know that I would choose just an ordinary day, a warm, summer day, perhaps, when, after we had watched the evening news together, as we always did, we would gather our dog, Annie, and scurry down to the dock, climb into our canoe and paddle the calm waters of the lake to watch the approaching sunset. I want to go back to just a beautiful, ordinary day with no extraordinary problems to think about and nothing particularly exciting going on in our lives. Just an ordinary day is the most precious moment in time.

THE SIXTH MONTH

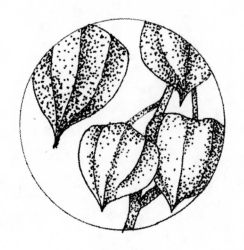

OCTOBER

I am beginning to realize that the road to healing is not a straight path upward, but rather a series of small steps leading to plateaus with several dips along the way. But my plateaus are definitely higher than they were. I am reaching out to people and wanting to go more places.

My friends in Atlanta have been urging me to visit them, and I fly there for a few days. To my surprise, I actually have a great time and do not feel like a third wheel with this couple. We're more like family. We do a lot of walking, talking, and reminiscing about David, and I find that I'm more easily able to talk about him without breaking down into a puddle of tears. We recall some humorous and cherished memories which span back over the forty years when David and I first met this couple onboard a ship. Before I leave Atlanta, they make me promise to visit them on a vacation trip they are planning this coming winter in California. I am starting to break out of my hard shell of loneliness.

When I return to Boston, I plan a dinner at my home for all the members of the bereavement group, so that we can gather together to watch an evening presidential election debate after our usual afternoon meeting. Six people come and we have a good time just getting to know one another in a more informal atmosphere, "breaking bread together," and talking politics. It feels so good to have a small crowd once again around the dining room table and in the living room.

My grandsons here in Boston keep reminding me of the impact their grandfather had on their lives. Noah, who is three, often picks up his toy phone and has imaginary conversations with his Poppy. He tells him we miss him, and asks him when he's going to return. Sometimes, he asks me if I want to talk to him on the phone. That really makes me take a deep breath and compose myself before I tell Noah, "Just send our love to Poppy and tell him we all miss him and love him." I've seen Noah go over to a photo of Poppy hanging on the wall and give him a huge smack on the lips. I have also done the same thing, and it makes me feel better. I have learned something from my three year old grandson. Jake illustrated a story he wrote about his Poppy and presented me recently with a hardbound book he published, called "Me and my Poppy." This is his way of showing how much he loved him and all the things he remembers doing with him. I am so touched by this book from my six year old grandson, and I place it in my treasure box.

Later this month, my niece, Jennifer, and I travel to Nantucket for a weekend of sightseeing. I've never been to this remote island, and we have a wonderful time together. I can't believe she got me to agree to pedal around the island on a tandem bicycle, but we spend a day bicycling, walking the beach, and visiting the vineyard on the island.

It's our last morning on the island, and we're sitting on a bench overlooking the harbor. I look up at the sky and ask Jennifer, "Am I imagining this or does it look as if all of the clouds are in a V formation?" She agrees they are but wonders why I am asking. "Because," I answer, "when David was dying, I told him to send me a sign in the shape of a V so I'll know he is out there somewhere and aware of my presence." We laugh and agree this must be David's signal to me. Strangely, I realize this is the first place on this earth to which I have traveled that David has never seen. Maybe, he *is* seeing it.

THE SEVENTH MONTH

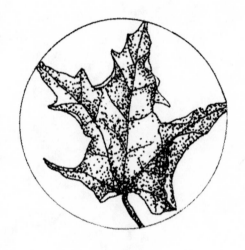

NOVEMBER

The flowers are all gone; the trees are bare. It's a rather gloomy time of the year, and Thanksgiving is coming up this month. How am I going to get through this holiday, one that used to be a favorite? Last year we had a huge gathering of family: the children, grandchildren, spouses, my brother and sister-in-law and most of their seven children, spouses, and grandchildren. They all came to Boston because we knew this would be David's last Thanksgiving.

I realize I must do something totally different and simple this year, so I gratefully accept an invitation to my son-in-law's parents' home for the holiday. Maybe, I have steeled myself for the occasion, but I am able to act cheerful and enjoy the holiday meal as a guest in a different setting from what I am used to. It isn't as though I don't think of who is missing from the holiday table, but I pull a temporary, gauzy shade down over the intrusive memories of last year, so that they are not as vivid or painful to me. Yet, by the end of the day, I say to myself, "I'm glad this *first* is over."

In our bereavement group we are all feeling a bit sadder as this time of year approaches with the ensuing holidays. I notice so many little things which make me sad or uncomfortable and add to the dips in the road on the way to healing. I find it startling just to browse through a greeting card aisle and suddenly be aware of so many cards which are no longer suitable for me to send: no more "*we* wish you…," "*both of us* send…," "to *our* daughter…," "happy birthday from the *two of us*…" or "from *our* house to yours." I'm now in a different category, no more *we* cards.

At our group meetings, we all discuss the little things which bother us, now that we are alone. We women feel the burden of doing all the little chores which were once our spouse's domain. Fixing anything around the house can become a monumental task; figuring out how to work a sophisticated remote control for the TV or VCR or a sound system can be daunting. I have a drawer filled with various remotes for which I can find no apparent use, and they do not seem to be affecting my existence at all! None of us wants to bother our family members for every minor task; we feel as if we're already a burden. One woman has moved just one house away from her daughter and son-in-law, and she says she refuses to bother them for every frustrating chore. I know I am sometimes perceived as ungrateful, demanding, or unappreciative, so I try to keep my requests to a minimum.

We women are also afraid of being alone in the house and falling or getting injured and not being able to call for help. We also are much more aware of our home security systems and use them at night when we're alone in the house. The men in our group have different problems, like not being adept at cooking. One keeps telling us about all the new ingredients he tries in his tuna fish salad to give it some variety. He says it jokingly, but I think that what he's expressing is not only his inexperience in the kitchen, but his sadness and solitude, especially at mealtime. These are all the minor, everyday problems we are each trying to work out as we muddle through life without our spouse at our side.

I feel frustrated, also, every time I have a medical question or apprehension about some ache or pain. David used to assuage my fears. I recently had to see an orthopedic doctor about a minor problem. The doctor took an x-ray and explained that it was an arthritic condition which could be alleviated by surgery. How I wish David could have looked at that x-ray and told me what to do! I opted to do nothing. The surgery sounded worse than the discomfort I sometimes feel. I hate making medical decisions without David's counsel.

I guess I sound whiny this month. It must be the time of year, and I'm feeling sorry for myself.

THE EIGHTH MONTH

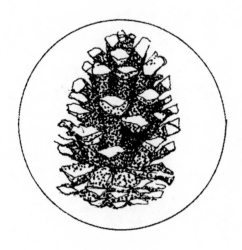

DECEMBER

This month, I am bracing myself not just for the cold, inclement weather which has started to descend upon Boston, but I'm bracing myself emotionally to withstand the time of year which I know will stir up a deep pot of memories. I have made plans to spend Chanukah in California and to bring in the New Year with a friend in Philadelphia.

The trip to California is fun. It's great to see the grandchildren, give gifts, take them to the movies, play games together and sleep in their bedrooms next to them. I need their affection as much as they need mine. Ariana and Alex spend time with me reminiscing and looking at photographs. They want to remember their Poppy, so we reflect back on the many things they did together when they used to visit us at the lake. Poppy taught Ari how to fish when she was just three years old, and she has the photo to prove it! Alex used to like to steer the big motor boat, and he shows me a picture of him and Poppy at the wheel. I hope my grandchildren will always carry these memories with them as they grow older. After several days, I return to Boston.

As I draw closer to the beginning of a new year, I feel some dissipation of the resentment and anger I have been harboring towards those friends who were not attentive enough to David in the course of his illness. I phone them, supposedly just to catch up on news and gossip and wish them a good New Year, but, really, I am calling to tell them, "You just couldn't cope well. You didn't know what to say to your dying friend, so you didn't come to his bedside. I'm disappointed, but I forgive you." Of course, those sentiments never actually got spoken during our conversations. Instead, we talked about the weather in upstate New York and Boston; we spoke about our children and grandchildren; we caught up on events in each other's lives. But, I'm glad I called. I know I'm healing inside.

It is packing time again, time for my end of the year visit to Philadelphia. On the plane, I recall New Year's Eve last year. It was such a psychological victory to me to be able to see David enter a new millenium. Entering the year 2000 made it *appear*, at least, that he was living a long time. After all, he was born in one century and would die in another. I'm glad to be out of town for this New Year.

Judy and I spend an afternoon and evening walking around Longwood Gardens near Philadelphia, taking in the beauty of the snowy landscape and the buildings decorated with a brilliant display of holiday lights and hundreds of poinsettia plants. It really is breathtaking, and I am enjoying my visit with a close friend.

For New Year's Eve, we attend a concert of the Philadelphia Orchestra. The Academy of Music in Philadelphia is an ornate, gorgeous, historic setting in which to hear beautiful music. I'm glad I made these plans. It's just that memories have a way of following me around no matter what city I'm in or in what setting. I listen to the melodious music and become teary-eyed, not just at the strains of music, but at the sight around me. It is New Year's Eve. Most of the audience is composed of couples, and, to put it simply, I envy them. After the concert,

Judy and I bring in the New Year with dessert and a toast to the future. My mind is on the past.

THE NINTH MONTH

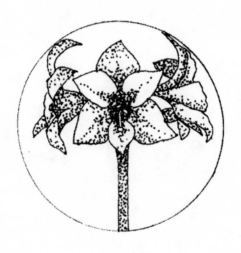

JANUARY

Finally, I had a dream about David, but it startled me, and I awoke from a disturbed sleep and had to consciously force myself to think about it, so that the images wouldn't suddenly vanish from my mind. It wasn't a pleasant dream, because in it David appeared healthy, smiling, and robust only for what seemed a few seconds; then he appeared gaunt, tired, and confused, as he was near the end of his life. My dream wasn't satisfying at all, as I had hoped. Maybe, another time. I wish I could write the script for it.

I continue to see Susan every week. She says I have stopped asking her, "How am I doing?" each week and have replaced it with "I know I am doing better." I guess I can see my own progress. I am much more interested in going to new places and meeting new people. I have gone to concerts and the ballet, and I hope to purchase tickets for a series of concerts next season. I'll order two tickets and take a friend each time.

I just met a neighbor who lives around the corner from me

and was going through the same, parallel experience as I. Helaine's husband was dying from cancer at the same time David was, and he also remained at home throughout his illness. Helaine, too, was the primary caregiver for her husband. How I wish I had known her two years ago. She has given me such a boost in my spirits, because she is outgoing, involved in the community, and inspirational in her outlook. She is just the friend I need. And to think she was living a few doors from me all this time!

This month I decide to give notice to my bereavement group that I intend to leave the group in February. I feel ready. I feel much stronger. The reactions from members of the group are interesting and varied. One person says, "You *think* you're strong, but *you'll* see. You will hit a low again. *I* did." Another agrees to a point. She says, "It is even harder the second year, because by then you *really* know he's not coming back, and you feel the absence even more." Someone else tells me she feels that she will get better at coping. "If *you* can do it, *I* can, too. You're an inspiration." One of the men remarks that he'll miss my insights and comments to the group, and he tells me he admires my fortitude.

As we go around the room and talk about our week, I realize that I am more upbeat than many of the others and better able to cope. I'm not sure why I have come this far so fast, but I have some idea. I have come to believe that my grieving started the day I found out that David was dying, not just since his death. In that respect, I feel that I have had more time than some in getting used to the idea of losing a loved one. We had nearly two years together after his diagnosis to talk about everything that was in our hearts. We spoke freely and frankly to each other about our concerns and deepest fears. We expressed our love for each other. Most importantly, we had time to say our "good-byes." For me, I know, in retrospect, that it helped to have this time together before he had to die. For David, though, I know it would have been much easier if he had died suddenly and could have avoided all those months of anxiety, fear, and pain, both physical and emotional.

I reflect back that during the course of David's illness, as he gradually became weaker, more confused, and helpless, I took

on the role of his ombudsman. I remember how I seemed to

grow stronger as he grew weaker, and I became more assertive

in directing the course of his treatment. Today, if I am strong

emotionally, it is in great part as a result of this role I had to

assume.

THE TENTH MONTH

FEBRUARY

It is hard to say goodbye to the bereavement group. We have all cried together and told each other our fears and our problems. I have exposed my heart in front of people who once were total strangers with just one common bond, that of loss. I say my good-byes by telling them how far I have come, yet how aware I am that I will have *down* days. Still, I am confident that I will bounce back from these and enter new, even higher plateaus. I feel a joy in living that I didn't feel ten months ago. I feel a resiliency. I'm ready to be on my own. Everyone hugs me, wishes me well, and makes me promise to keep in touch and report back to the group.

It is mid February and once again I am putting Annie into a kennel so that I can travel to California for a quick visit with the family there and a California vacation with my friends from Atlanta. Annie has been to the kennel just about a week out of each month since David's death, because of all the traveling I have been doing.

I am vacationing in the California desert when I receive a phone call telling me that Annie has suddenly died. She just went to sleep one night and never awoke. No sign of a problem. No warning. I am stunned and weepy and very sad, once again. The *down* days have arrived again all too soon. This time, I feel guilty. How could her heart have just stopped? Did I miss some sign of a heart problem? She was sleeping a lot, but that's what older dogs do. I hadn't noticed anything. She had been there for David to comfort him throughout his illness, and she had been there through the first ten months of my bereavement, when *I* needed her. Now, she's gone. I'm so glad to be with friends at this time. They are comforting to me and realize I need to cry and talk and just have some quiet time for reflection. After a couple of days, I'm much better, not as *down*. I *am* more resilient. I loved that little dog so much. Yet, I'm going to be all right.

When I return to Boston, I notice a huge difference in the house. Now, it's *really* empty. I am so used to walking into the house and talking to Annie. I find I am not using my voice unless I'm on the phone. Sometimes, I make a conscious effort to talk aloud in my house just to break the silence. Now, for the first time, I am totally alone with no one to care for but myself.

THE ELEVENTH MONTH

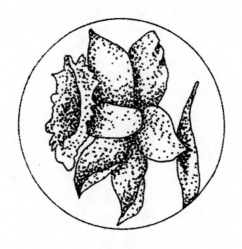

MARCH

I have settled into a pleasant routine. Twice a week I baby-sit for Noah, so that my daughter can teach art part- time at a high school nearby. Heidi is grateful to me for helping out, but the benefit is just as rewarding to me. I have formed such a strong bond with this little guy and love it when he tells his mommy to please leave the house, so we can be alone together.

Some days I meet a friend for a movie or dinner. Some days I work at my computer, trying to become more computer literate. I have learned that I can order books on-line and can even buy local movie tickets at some theatres. I am also learning how to do word processing and send e-mails. I'm proud of my new skills!

I also joined a gym and try to do a mild workout at least twice a week. My health is more important to me now, and I make sure that I cook healthful, well balanced meals, even if it is just for one. Sometimes, I ask a friend to join me for dinner. I am making an effort to eat at normal times, because, being alone, I have the urge to eat earlier than the usual dinner hours.

This month I travel to Sarasota, on the west coast of Florida, for a spring vacation with Heidi, Phil, and the boys. It is my first time staying at a beach since David died. He had always loved this particular Gulf area of Florida, because he had been stationed in Tampa while he was in the Air Force, and Heidi was born in Florida. I am surprised at how much I can enjoy myself, even though I am reminded of David as I travel these familiar roads. But I am beginning to think of him more and more with a smile on my face, ready to relate some amusing story about him.

I visit some retired friends while in this area, and my girl-friend asks me if I am making new friends in Boston. I reply, "Yes, I've made a few wonderful friends." She then asks, "Are they all widows?" I reply, "For the most part, yes. Couples don't usually invite a single person to join them. Do *you* invite any widows when you go out socially or have a party at your house?" She has to admit the answer is "no." I realize I'm in a special category now, and unless I'm with longtime friends who knew me when I was married, I probably won't be asked to many social events given by married people. I think back and wonder if I was sensitive enough to this issue when I was a "couple."

I attend a wedding the last weekend of this month. I am seated at a table with couples. I find it a refreshing and pleasant surprise not to be seated at a "widow's table." It is a bit awkward when couples get up to dance, but usually one or two couples remain at the table for conversation, and one time during the reception my friend comes over to ask me to dance with him. I have a good time at the wedding. It feels *almost* normal.

I have had only one or two more dreams about David, and, to be honest, they were unremarkable in that I couldn't even remember them. I remember only that he traveled through my mind fleetingly and then was gone. Again, I can't say it was satisfying, and I still can't figure out why more images of him don't appear in my dreams, when he filled up my life for so many years.

THE TWELFTH MONTH

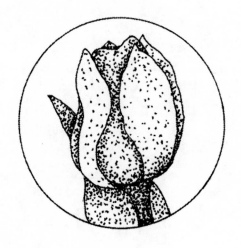

APRIL

The tulip bulbs I planted last fall are erupting from the ground. I see signs of spring all over to remind me once again of the renewal of life. Yet, this is the first year anniversary of David's death.

I know I will mark the anniversary of his death in a special way. I have made a memorial garden for David in my patio area, and in it I have put some of my favorite perennials, including a white phlox named "David" and white bleeding hearts. Most of the garden is white, but I also added some blue flowers, like forget-me-nots and corydalis. This morning I placed a stone in the garden. On it is etched the word "remember."

Last night, Heidi and I attended synagogue services and said *Kaddish*, a special memorial prayer. We have also each illuminated a memorial light in our homes which will remain on until sunset tonight, the official end of the day in the Jewish religion. Susan rings my doorbell this morning to hand me a

bouquet of roses and a note. I am so moved that she remem-
bered David's anniversary and would stop over to see how I'm
doing and to give me a hug. I show her the memorial garden I
have planted.

It is necessary for Heidi and me to attend a good friend's
bridal shower this afternoon for a few hours. We sit through the
luncheon and the opening of some gifts, but I keep glancing at
my watch and getting jittery as the minutes approach the time
when David died last year. About five minutes before three
o'clock, I squeeze Heidi's hand and quietly leave the room and
find my way to the bathroom.

This time, I cannot keep the intrusive memories away; nor
do I want to. I begin to relive the final moments of David's life:
I have flashbacks of my stroking him and telling him how much
I love him and will love him for eternity. I keep talking to him
and touching him until the nurse tells me he is gone, and then I
give him one final kiss. Here, in this bathroom of a stranger's
house, I am sobbing softly and moaning with fresh felt memories. After about fifteen minutes, I wash my face, compose

myself, and rejoin the group for a few minutes before Heidi and I excuse ourselves to go home.

Heidi and I spend the evening together. Tonight, we're not hungry, but we decide to bring in some Chinese hot and sour soup for our dinner, the same kind of soup that David loved. The two of us sit at the kitchen table, eating our bowls of soup, talking about David, and thinking he would highly approve of this meal to mark his day.

Before I go to bed, I unplug the memorial light and feel both guilty and sad doing so. I know that, even though a year has passed since David's death, my mourning isn't over. Extinguishing a light doesn't mean I have extinguished the memory. I will carry David's memory with me as I continue on with my living.

Susan asked me recently if it has felt like a year has passed. I said that in some ways it seems like just a short while ago, because I have been so occupied with paperwork and other matters to take up my time. But in most ways, it seems so much longer than a year; it especially seems ages since I last spoke with him or touched him. I have only to gaze at the photo on my desk to realize how entirely different my current life is. It's a photo taken four years ago on the Fourth of July in Cazenovia. In it, David and I are dressed up in matching red and white, flag- striped vests, and David is holding Annie. I can't believe so much has changed so suddenly: no more husband, no more dog, no more house, no more lake. I hate the words *no more*!

I have gotten through all the important *firsts* this year: the first father's day without him, the first Fourth of July, the first Thanksgiving, and all the others. Yet, I know there will still be other *firsts* in other years. There are always markers in life.

But I feel his strength inside of me, and I am gazing ahead toward the future, not always looking back, as I did in the beginning. The emotional pain I felt in the first few months is not as severe, and the painful images are not as vivid. It's as if I've covered them over with a piece of gauze. I'm stronger; I'm tougher; and in so many ways, I'm a better, more empathetic, more forgiving, and wiser person than I ever was. Thank you, David.

Birth is a beginning
And death a destination.
And life is a journey:
From childhood to maturity
And youth to age;
From innocence to awareness
And ignorance to knowing;
From foolishness to discretion
And then, perhaps, to wisdom;
From weakness to strength
Or strength to weakness —
And, often, back again;
From health to sickness
And back, we pray, to health again;
From offense to forgiveness,
From loneliness to love,
From joy to gratitude,
From pain to compassion,
And grief to understanding —
From fear to faith;
From defeat to defeat to defeat —
Until, looking backward or ahead,
We see that victory lies
Not at some high place along the way,
But in having made the journey, stage by stage,
A sacred pilgrimage.
Birth is a beginning
And death a destination.
And life is a journey,
A sacred pilgrimage —
To life everlasting.

Yom Kippur prayer read at Kol Nidre.

ABOUT THE AUTHOR

Barbara Cheris is a native of Syracuse, New York where she raised her family. She received a B.A. in English education and a M.S. in education from Syracuse University, as well as an Ed.S. from the University of Michigan and is a former reading specialist. She was married for forty-two years to David Cheris, M.D., a radiologist. She currently resides in Newton, Massachusetts.